CATCHING

Broken

FISH

CATCHING *Broken* FISH

UNTANGLING DISCIPLESHIP
FROM A TRACTOR SEAT

MATTHEW STEWART SIMON

REDEMPTION
PRESS

Published by Redemption Press, PO Box 427, Enumclaw, WA 98022.

Toll-Free (844) 2REDEEM (273-3336)

Redemption Press is honored to present this title in partnership with the author. The views expressed or implied in this work are those of the author. Redemption Press provides our imprint seal representing design excellence, creative content, and high-quality production.

The author has tried to recreate events, locales, and conversations from memories of them. In order to maintain their anonymity, in some instances the names of individuals, some identifying characteristics, and some details may have been changed, such as physical properties, occupations, and places of residence.

ISBN 13: 978-1-64645-292-7 (Paperback)
978-1-64645-293-4 (ePub)
978-1-64645-294-1 (Mobi)

Library of Congress Catalog Card Number: 2021910129

For my mother, for her relentless pursuit of me. For her dedication to the development of my character and to my salvation. I am so grateful.

And for my wife, Jeana, who has persevered with me, shown me kindness and grace, and always believed in me. You are forever my favorite.

Author's Note

I never had any intentions of being a writer. I am not a gleaming example of extraordinary faith. I have not spent my life scouring every inch of my Bible. There is nothing exceptional about my upbringing or my life's pursuits. This book is about what salvation and discipleship look like to me. My hope is that you read it from the place I wrote it—a place of humility and thankfulness for God's hand on my life.

As a farmer, I have learned about nurture, about God and his powerful metaphors, and about how his creation speaks his Word to us. From the unseen microbes of the soil to the beauty of crops of grain at harvest, his lessons are all around us. We need only humble ourselves and press our ears toward him.

These are the lessons I have learned, the few of his many that I have grasped wholly and understood when he has made them plain to me.

My life and its examples are neither a proclamation of wisdom nor a statement of judgment. They are, more reliably, a product of failure and growth. If God can love me, he most certainly loves you. I only hope to inspire you to change the world around you.

Bountiful Waters

WHAT DOES YOUR HEART SAY ABOUT the world we live in? There are so many shootings, conflicts, and wars, so much violence and cruelty. What makes someone desperate enough to take another's life? What will it take to make it stop? Our society is suffering, and no amount of regulation, no amount of legislation will heal it. Do you think our government has the answer?

Here is the answer, laid out in black and white: it is what *we* choose to do, not what our politicians legislate. It is the choices you and I make. This answer is the same as it has always been and the same as it will always be. It is the answer that brings people to know and love God as we do. It is the answer that heals people from the inside out. It is the way we must live and speak and give and love. This answer is the reason the Bible is eternally relevant. It is the way we reach people. "Follow me," Jesus said, "and I will make you fishers of men" (Matthew 4:19 NIV). Jesus was talking about making *us* teachers, making us living, walking examples of God's love.

To begin, we must establish what it is we want for others. A goal, something to strive to achieve. I may be the most blessed person on earth. I have everything I really need. No, I am not rich. But I am married to an amazing woman. She is kind, patient, and has nearly never-ending grace for me. I don't know anyone who is more hard-working and more beautiful. I have an amazing marriage, a great family, smart kids, beautiful sisters, and loving parents. We have our share of struggles, dysfunction, and strife, but only a fool would trade what I have for anything else.

My goal is for others to be as blessed as I am. What I want is to share this life with others. So how do I show them how to have what I have? Not *my* exact life, but a unique version that has meaning and purpose for them. How do I show them this life of abundance? How do we help someone else get from there to here? It starts with understanding the paradigm of others and gains momentum and power from the words we choose.

Words are the most powerful force in the universe. We Christians believe that the universe began with them. They precede and end nearly every conflict, either personal or global. They mend broken hearts, change minds, provoke laughter, or bring tears. They start wars, draw boundaries, and make declarations. Our civilization will rise and fall with them. Your choice of words will determine your fate and the fate of those around you. How will you use them?

More than ever, we live in a world in constant conflict, an infinite battleground of dysfunction, bountiful waters for those who would look to promote Christ's message to heal people and revive God's mission on earth. Your choice to encourage, unite, and heal others is essential to changing the path and destiny of the world.

Before we begin, some realizations must be made. We are all broken. We each have tragedies, disappointments, and losses that have shaped us. Each of us is in a unique place on our journey of understanding and faith. So let me thank you in advance for your commitment to change and growth, without which we cannot prevail. Together we are the people, those rare individuals with the heart and aptitude for catching broken fish.

PART 1

Learning to Fish

TO EMBRACE GOD IS TO EMBRACE change. We are born into sin. Change, for the sake of discipleship, requires the abandonment of ungodly principles and concepts we have used to construct our identity. The choice to let go of our own motives and personal beliefs and begin comparing our own words and actions to the character of Jesus Christ leads us to God. We grow like a plant, varying our rate of maturity with the seasons, understanding the benefits of both the warm sunshine and the cold rain. Discipleship is that growth, constantly seeking how to better ourselves and reach God's broken people. It is not a destination at which we arrive, but rather a journey and road we humbly travel. I have learned to embrace and celebrate this kind of change, even though at times I still futilely resist it. As a father I pray that my children would grow and become better. I believe it to be what our Father in heaven requires of us as well.

CHAPTER 1

Mindsets

I AM A FARMER. FOR THE last ten years of my life, I have spent my summers making hay near the shores of Lake Michigan. The rest of the year I am a bus driver for the local school district. And though I have had many professions, these two jobs have changed and challenged me the most. At a minimum, they have made me more humble, and sure of God's grace. Nothing I have experienced will temper a man's steel more than farming, and I cannot imagine two professions that will make you wake up in the morning, look in the mirror, and say, "Why am I doing this?" more than these. Each spring I, and other farmers, put thousands of dollars into the ground, hoping and praying for a return. We put our faith in God and, to a lesser extent, the weatherman on the line every year. My return on that investment can be measured each fall with the thankfulness of having a full barn and the relief of "just driving a bus" for a while.

To what degree are you thankful? As a farmer, could you be thankful for the smallest bit of rain after weeks of drought? Could you find a way to be thankful when you are starting over again after frost killed the corn you just planted? Could you be thankful you have the right clothes to work all day in wind chills ten degrees below zero?

We in the United States have become accustomed to abundance, so much so that we don't even recognize it. We look at our homes as not big enough and our cars as not new enough. In order to change the world and influence those who need us, we may want to snap out of it. So how do we have that change of heart? We learn to recognize abundance.

Let's start with the obvious. Where were you born? A war-torn third-world country? Probably not. Have you ever gone without meals, clothing, or shelter? Have you ever lived in a place where there was no power or indoor plumbing? Have you lived where you had to boil your drinking water? Most of us can answer no to those questions. So how do we recognize abundance?

The short answer is *service*—after all, Jesus came to serve, not to be served. When we follow his example, when we serve people less fortunate than we are, it changes us. Not sure about this? Volunteer at a soup kitchen or homeless shelter. Offer your service to help people rebuild after a hurricane or tornado. Better still, go on a mission trip to Haiti or Honduras or to a region where people live in squalor. I have seen entire mission groups leave the country with suitcases full of clothes and come back with only the shirts on their backs. Why? Because they left to change the world and came home with a change of heart. They came back understanding the extent of the abundance that we in America enjoy every day. Their eyes have been opened to see and understand what it's like for people to live with almost nothing.

Serving is indeed what makes us humble, what allows us to see that we have been given a gift. Think of the things you did nothing to earn: your looks, your intelligence, your strength, or the country where you were born. Think of the good fortune and blessing to be able to read and write and express yourself as if somehow these things were guaranteed. Recognize that not everyone was given what we were given—the full realization of which leads us to a place of humility and ultimately kindness and grace.

> When we follow his example, when we serve people less fortunate than we are, it changes us.

These are the questions to ask ourselves:

Am I convinced I live in abundance?

Am I thankful and content with what I have?

Am I humble?

Do I know what it means to have a heart for people?

Am I ready to respond to people with compassion and kindness?

Can I expect people who come from a place of dependency or depravity to exhibit the same behavior as I do?

Psalm 23:5 (KJV) says, "Thou preparest a table before me in the presence of mine enemies; thou anointest my head with oil; *my cup runneth over*" (emphasis added). Until the day we meet God face to face, I am not sure we will ever understand the meaning or gravity of this passage to the extent of its intention. We witness God's abundance for us daily but often fail to recognize it. This very concept occurred to me one day in an amazing way. That epiphany is memorialized in the following story.

CASTING THE LINE

One November day at ten in the morning, I was talking to my wife, Jeana, on the phone. As she stepped into her car to head for her next meeting, she realized our daughter had left her lunch behind. Knowing she would be pressed for time if she had to swing back to the high school to give it to Madison, Jeana opened the bag and rattled off the components of Madison's cold lunch. Within fifteen minutes I had a new one assembled and brought to the school's front office.

Later that day, Madison thanked me and revealed that she didn't realize she had left it behind until the secretary at the school informed her. She went on about how her mother and I spoil her and how well we take care of her, even when she doesn't realize how we are working behind the scenes. It was a great conversation, and I talked to her about how it made her feel and how she could do this for others.

But the next morning I awoke at 4:00 a.m., and as I lay in bed, I was struck with an epiphany. On the brink of Thanksgiving, I was amused at how plain God had made his lesson to me.

I am providing for you always. I could clearly hear his voice in my head. Humbled, I went on with my morning rituals, listening more intently for the details of God's sermon to me that day. I reflected on my life and was amazed again at where his path has led me, where he has made so many exceptions to allow for my faults and weaknesses. Truly I will never know the extent of his grace and providence for me. I will never understand how much he is working behind the scenes in my life. Certainly, I can never anticipate the next "cold lunch" he will have waiting for me when I don't even realize I have left it behind.

This Thanksgiving I hope to sit down at a table full of great food and—with people I love and with more humility than ever—understand his providence. Between now and next Thanksgiving, I pray that I would hear and comprehend his love for me even more. And more importantly, that I would show others his providence for them.

PRAYER FOR CHANGE

God, today and always, please forgive me for not thanking you enough for the unseen ways you work in my life. Please help me to express your love by showing others your providence in my life. I know there is no better way to show you how thankful I am. Amen.

CHAPTER 2
Behavior

WE BROUGHT HOME A NEW RESCUE dog recently, a fiery little blue heeler named Pepper. Pepper was a mess until a nice lady found her living in an old horse trailer and saved her. She had fleas, lice, and a yeast infection all over her body. Some of her fur was missing, and you could see her ribs because she was extremely underweight. In the first month she was in our home, she bit our old hound dog on the ear and entangled herself in a good scrap with our cat. At night we use safety gates to barricade her in her own room. She was insecure around us and wouldn't ever bark. You could easily see her anxiety. It didn't take us long to realize why she was so aggressive with our other pets. The conditions of her previous life were the only things she knew. Having little or nothing to eat was her normal, so she would be aggressive about food and even try to bury anything extra under the rug. In her mind she was still fighting to survive.

It took a little time, but needless to say, she acts differently now. She has started to understand that she now lives in abundance, and while she occasionally growls at the hound and keeps her distance from the cat, she gets along with them pretty well. Pepper craves attention—I think the concept of love was foreign to her before, but she can't get enough of it now. And this family loves her too. We understand why she is the way she is, and while we have changed the conditions she lives in now, we can still tell where she came from.

So what is your normal? Is it the same as everyone else's? Even if you grew up in an average, loving, and functional family, do you think most other people did?

The conditions that exist in our personal lives are indeed *ours*. They create a bias, a bias we don't even think we have. The scope of who we are based on the conditions of our life is so vast. Each individual experience, each moment changes us—the place where we grew up, the country, the state, city, neighborhood, and household.

Being the same as anyone else is a virtual impossibility, and we should be thankful for that. Think of how meaningless and boring life would be if we were exactly the same. Shouldn't we celebrate the diversity in our family, our country, and our world?

So there are some clear reasons why we act the way we do. Some of them, like in Pepper's case, are the conditions surrounding the way we grew up. Others' life experiences may include abuse, neglect, or absence of a positive role model (or the presence of a poor one). If you look closely, you can see these behaviors in others. You can hear the harsh tone in the voice of someone who was verbally abused, or maybe see them avoid confrontation all together. You may sometimes perceive it in a child who acts out for attention because he or she is nearly invisible at home.

> If we understand that conditions beyond our control dictate our choices of words and actions, can we move beyond blame and see people how God sees them? Can we love the sinner and hate the sin?

With this in mind, does it really make sense to blame people for who they are? If we understand that conditions beyond our control dictate our choices of words and actions, can we move beyond blame and see people how God sees them? Can we love the sinner and hate the sin?

We can, and we can do so with compassion and purpose. We can help people break the cycle that has brought them to a place of dysfunction. We can help people grow, which in turn fosters growth in ourselves. We can become "fishers of men"; we can catch the broken fish and show them God's path to becoming whole again. That process begins with seeing the brokenness of each of us. It begins with putting ourselves in their place and seeing them how God sees them. It begins with gaining their unique viewpoint.

CASTING THE LINE

My wife and I are a bit of an anomaly. In a typical relationship, a man ranks being respected as a priority, while women often gravitate toward a need for an emotional connection (love). To say we are typical would be far from the truth. While my wife can be emotional at times, her strength is in her ability to complete tasks, and she finds serving people, by outworking everyone else, to be her forte. She feels respected when she works harder than anyone else. Results matter, but the amount of effort put forth is most important. She is good at almost everything. To tease her I often say, "Imagine living in your shadow like I have too." Once, on our way home from vacation, I wanted her to experience driving the truck while pulling the fifth-wheel trailer. She hesitated but eventually said she would drive, which put me in the passenger's seat. I have a keen sense of direction and require little navigational assistance while driving, but if she has a weak suit, sense of direction it is! In a lapse of good judgment, and in front of the entire family, I made some poor choices about teasing her about this weakness. In a rare moment, she became emotional.

I was in trouble. How could someone so strong be so insecure? Easy answer: What I said was disrespectful. I made fun of her in the worst way possible. In a moment of genius, I recovered. "If you were good at everything, what would you need me for?" I said. "Do you know what it's like living with someone who works as hard as you?"

She giggled. I knew I had said the right thing.

Jeana and I have processed together many of the reasons we function the way we do. We know from where most of our insecurities come. We are broken, even though she and I have learned to function and even thrive with our inadequacies. I believe this is why we pair so well together. We have even matured to the point of making light of our faults at times. One day, in a moment of humility, I asked her to say, when I'm insecure about our relationship, "I love you, stupid." Why? When I act like I am unsure of her love for me, I am acting stupid.

Since then I have been able to wean myself from some insecurities. It started with understanding myself, revealing my weakness to her, and eventually handing that insecurity over to God.

Are you able to recognize your own less-than-desirable behavior? What insecurities drive these words or actions? Do you think understanding them would foster your own growth and change?

PRAYER FOR CHANGE

God, thank you for helping me to recognize the reasons for my own behavior. Help me to see others how you see them by recognizing their struggles in the words and actions they choose. Help me to love them like you love them and separate their heart from their poor choices. Not to change them, but to understand them. Amen

CHAPTER 3

Perspective

IT'S LATE AT NIGHT, AND YOU are driving home on a country road. In the distance you see a single headlight. It's coming straight at you as you reach your turn. It's hard to tell if it's a motorcycle or a car with a broken headlight. You feel uncertain about how far away it is, so you hesitate. You realize thirty seconds later that you could have easily made your turn in time.

What was missing?

Perspective.

The car's second headlight helps us calculate distance. In fact, your brain likely analyzes, calculates, and executes thousands of reliable decisions every day based on perspective. That function is critical to our survival and equally important in our relationships. Truly learning a different perspective gives us the data required for good judgment, and it is essential to obtaining wisdom. What is the formula for wisdom?

I think it looks like this:

$$knowledge + experience + perspective = wisdom$$

I am in constant pursuit of wisdom. In my opinion, wise people tend to have the greatest impact on the world around them, with the smallest effort. Out of the three parts of this equation, perspective is easily the most available yet least utilized.

People are almost constantly giving you their perspective—if you are listening. How well do you listen? Do you listen to the inflection in a person's voice? Are you reading their body language? Do you see their emotions in their language? Are you equipped to make a wise response? Do you jump to answer without comprehending and truly understanding their perspective? Are you really gaining perspective?

The value of perspective is so often overlooked. It hides in the shadows, waiting to make a fool of us.

Just the other day while I was driving the school bus, a boy who had a reputation for being a little rough gave a young girl a bloody nose. The students nearby reported that he had hit her. I rushed to her aid and then to his immediate judgment. I scolded the boy and told him he needed to sit in the front. My *knowledge* of him and my *experience* with him led me to believe that my judgment was sound. Later when teachers investigated, they found that the boy and girl had accidentally hit head to head. I offered that young man my apology the next day, but apologies are poor substitutes for good judgment.

> Crafting the lens that people see you through is an art that combines gaining people's perspective as well as investing in them.

My failure to pursue his perspective turned my opportunity to be wise into folly. I assumed I knew the truth, and we all know where assumptions lead us. They certainly, at a minimum, may lead us to feeling guilty. At best they will lead us to apologize.

So taking time to gain the perspective of others is paramount to sound judgment and wisdom, but what about the perception people have of us? I call these types of perspective "lenses," and they are important if you want to have influence. Crafting the lens that people see you through is an art that combines gaining people's perspective as well as investing in them.

CASTING THE LINE

I have a friend I have known for thirty years. I don't know what it is that we share in common really. She isn't even a close friend or someone I talk to often. Her family and mine have different views. In fact, a good part of her family is vegan, and I'm a beef farmer.

The other day she sent me a video about a farmer who married a vegan woman, who eventually bought his cattle and turned them into pets. It was a cool story and I enjoyed it.

My friend thought it was a cute story, but I felt she did this in an effort to bring me over to her way of thinking. I could have been offended, but I wasn't. If some stranger had done the same, I may have told him to get lost, or maybe I wouldn't even have watched the video. But instead my friend and I had a great conversation.

So that got me thinking, *Why is my response different with her?*

The answer is simple. In the thirty years I've known her, she has shown me that she cares about me and wants only good for me and my family. She has said the things that have crafted the lens that I see her through. It is that lens that softens edges, ends indifference, and builds bridges.

There is no fairy-tale ending to this story, and I didn't become a vegan. But I will always listen when she talks, even if I think she's gone crazy.

In truth I have many friends and family that fit this description— people who have taken the time to craft a lens for me—and I value it so much and love them all.

The world will change when we all take the time to craft a lens with others we meet and when we use that influence to help each other.

Think about the lenses you are crafting today, the words you are saying, the influence you could have on those who love you.

This is what Jesus was doing, and his love still has influence two thousand years later.

Read that last line again: This is what Jesus was doing, and his love still has influence two thousand years later. Think about it—what

> The world will change when we all take the time to craft a lens with others we meet and when we use that influence to help each other.

better way to change the world? If we only emulated his ability to compassionately gain perspective and craft a lens, our impact would be huge!

Investing in each other is what binds us together and makes us great. Gaining perspective is what amplifies our capacity to disciple people. Together, investment and perspective are the door to influence and the catalyst for change. Individually and collectively, they project our love to others. They set the stage for us to influence others in the most positive way.

PRAYER FOR CHANGE

God, help me to listen well and to avoid assuming the perspective of others. Help me to understand the paradigm that is unique to them. Please give me the patience to craft the lenses that others see me through, lenses that are the product of learning to understand and invest in other broken people. Amen

CHAPTER 4

Influence

LAST YEAR MY WIFE SURPRISED ME with some Eric Church concert tickets. He is probably my favorite country artist. His concerts are amazing—so much so that he won the 2020 CMA Entertainer of the Year award. People often speak about the influence that a popular singer, performer, or athlete can have on the world. But why is it that they can have so much more of an impact? Are they smarter or wiser than you and me? Chances are they are not, but they have done something to bring people together, and that by itself is powerful.

We've all enjoyed that feeling of having a great singer or songwriter bring us back to a place or a time with just a few notes, and we've watched that amazing Olympic athlete unite an entire nation with their inspiring performances. So how do they do it? Is it something they create? The answer may be that what they do is simply uplifting. Their words or actions make us feel inspired, hopeful, or proud. They inspire love, or joy, or a feeling of accomplishment. Either purposefully or accidentally they have painted a picture that many of us enjoy, and through it their popularity and influence grows. This influence gives them an opportunity to change the world. People listen when they speak, and people will listen to you as well, provided you choose words that inspire and encourage them.

Here's a perfect example of how we can lose our influence and ability to foster change. It's an example that is right in front of us every day: the misuse of social media. I don't know if the devil himself could create a better way to alienate and offend people.

I read some posts and think to myself, *If you had to say the same words to people face to face, would you do it?* My daughter made me laugh the other day when she said, "Shouldn't it really be called Hiding-Your-Face Book?"

I've seen it so many times: a well-written and factually sound post, usually political and almost always cynical, a scalding, critical look at the actions or opinions of others. The comments and likes tell the story. Almost without exception this post will be seen by the same ten or twenty people who share the same viewpoint. A follow-up to the author's page will most likely reveal that he or she is followed by a scant few. Rarely will the post be shared, and the net change in the world will be negligible. Any truth will be lost in a sea of pessimism.

> People want the truth given to them in a way that is uplifting.

Why does the post fail to have impact? Some would say that people don't want to hear the truth. I disagree. People want the truth given to them in a way that is uplifting. Think of how we interact with children. If we must break bad news to them, we often try to show the up side.

CASTING THE LINE

When your old dog or pet passes on, you tell your children he has lived a good life or express how he is no longer in pain. We often spare few words to help them feel less emotional. Maybe we believe adults should not need this same level of empathy, but somehow we have failed to recognize the importance of those caring words.

As adults we forgo many of the kindnesses that we grant to children. If we make a habit out of responding this way, our influence with the people around us will wane. "They should know better," "Sorry for being blunt," and "I'm just being honest" are phrases that come to mind. But truth without the benefit of love is discipline without purpose. So why is the compassionate use of our words so important?

> Service is the Reset button. It remains the most effective tool for changing your heart and will create an opportunity for personal growth and change.

It is important because we as humans are more or less an equation, and even though we are each born with a unique and infinite number of variables between birth and death, God has made us in his image. Our paths run parallel to each other. These paths intersect at intervals, like rungs on a ladder. These rungs unite us and hold us together. They are what we share, common values and goals.

We all, with little exception, subconsciously reject the correction that comes from others' pessimism and negativity, even if it contains the truth. Most times without even recognizing it. We aspire to be loved and respected. We embrace kindness and mercy. It is the erosion of those values that leads us to negativity and to treat others in ways we know we shouldn't. Usually, these words come when we are under stress or feel poorly about ourselves. Cynicism usually starts a cycle of criticism—which we must recognize and reject if we hope to have any meaningful influence on the people and the world around us.

I am guilty of this kind of negativity at times. But I have trained myself to recognize the nonverbal cues that people give me when I am being negative and cynical. Even still, I have my moments when the world has me where it wants me. In these moments, I can count on my friends and family to hear me out when I am on a rant, because they love me, but I can see it in their eyes when I have become too jaded.

If we are to have influence and bring change to the world, we must reject negativity and cynicism. They close more doors than they open. There is no better way to camouflage yourself in the world and lose your influence with people. With Jesus, the path to influence and change leads in the opposite direction. If you find yourself being cynical or pessimistic about people, return to serving others. Service is the Reset button. It remains the most effective tool for changing your heart and will create an opportunity for personal growth and change.

So how can we tell when we have chosen the right words to say? If you have truly gained perspective, if you have taken the time to craft a lens, if you have created a relationship of trust, compassion, and understanding, you are on the right track to choosing the words that will influence others. How do I know this? Because Jesus modeled it for us. He sees the value in each of us and understands our behavior perfectly. He has never-ending patience and grace for us, invests in us daily, and made the ultimate sacrifice for us. To put it simply, he has defined love in its most pure form.

PRAYER FOR CHANGE

God, please help me to choose my words carefully. Help me to inspire people to change in the way that you have inspired me. Help me to reject my negative and cynical thoughts, and replace them with patience, even when I am frustrated. Increase my influence with others. Amen

✣ CHAPTER 5

Investment

THERE ARE SO MANY WAYS THAT people perceive love. We can encourage, sacrifice, listen, and give gifts. We can open our homes to people, share food with them, and work beside them. Sometimes it's as simple as picking up the phone and letting someone know you are thinking about them. When you boil them all down, it comes down to investment. When you spend time or resources caring for someone else, people perceive it as love.

During this past winter, my sister and I signed up at a local gym. We wanted to try to hit this spring a little lighter and a little stronger. For me, indoor cardio is about the most boring thing in the world, and through a process of elimination we decided it would be the most beneficial if we rode stationary bikes for part of our workouts. The gym has one of those movie screens that drop down and videos that guide you through various prerecorded workouts.

One morning I arrived to see that someone had already chosen a workout and was ready to start her ride. I'd had a brief conversation with her weeks ago, and she quickly volunteered that it would be fine if I joined her. I set up my bike some distance away from her but close enough that I could still see the screen. I thought this would save me embarrassment if I could not keep up on the hour-long ride. Vanessa had other plans.

You see, even though I had distanced myself physically from her, in her mind we were riding "together."

Twenty minutes later, during one of the more grueling portions, my performance waned. I would have been content to lower the resistance, sit up tall, coast out the rest of the section, and resume when I caught my breath. It was in that moment that this woman, whom I hardly know, looked over at me and yelled, "Don't quit. Come on!" Without hesitation I stood up on the pedals, mashed them down, and pushed myself again.

Two thoughts crowded my mind: *I don't even know this lady. What does she think she is doing, talking to me this way?* and *Man, I am glad she is here to motivate me.* It was then that Vanessa became affectionately known as "the punisher." We became fast friends.

My sister and I often ride or workout with the punisher nowadays. Even though I now count her as a good friend, I still think she enjoys seeing me in pain. Vanessa is an encourager. She invests in people every day. Everyone at the gym loves her, and they often join her in "encouraging" me, much to my chagrin. There is no doubt that she loves people and enjoys bringing out the best in them. If she gets a chance to cheer you on to victory, she will, and I am thankful for her.

Maybe, though not to the same degree, I am an encourager too. Some weeks I feel as though that's all I do. I find it to be one of the easiest ways to support and invest in people. Your words of encouragement are a gift, one you can give people in just a few seconds that may make all the difference. It seems so ironic that we will cheer or even scream for our favorite artist or sports team, but we rarely say a single word of encouragement to the people we profess to love when the impact could be so dramatic. Think of how easy it is to tell someone, "You got this!" or to support the good behavior of a child by saying, "Well done."

Prayer is the most amazing form of investment.

In truth, I believe encouragement all by itself can change the world. It is a powerful tool. I could easily write an entire book on the power of it. Why do you think in sports, the home team wins more often?

At some level, encouragement has shaped us into what we are today, because someone took the time to say "You got this!" or in my case, "Don't quit. Come on!"

If you want people to love you and follow you, if you want to be a leader and a fisher of men, learn to spot opportunities to encourage. It is one of the most life-changing and inspiring forms of love.

To me, prayer is the most amazing form of investment. We can pray for those who would accept no other form of love from us. We can pray for our enemies. We can pray for our own heart to change or to see someone in a different light. We can pray for wisdom and God's perspective.

When we pray, we align ourselves to receive God's blessings. The Bible says, "If my people, which are called by my name, shall humble themselves, and pray, and seek my face, and turn from their wicked ways; then will I hear from heaven, and will forgive their sin, and will heal their land" (2 Chronicles 7:14 KJV).

Is this not what this entire book is about? Humility, seeking God's ways, healing our nation and our world? Offered freely to us if only we would humble ourselves and pray.

Loving people financially can be perilous but also full of blessings. Giving things is generally more successful than giving cash, and it is best done with complete strangers. Familiarity between the giver and receiver often leads to resentment. God has blessed me as both a giver and receiver.

CASTING THE LINE

I had an old Honda Civic that I drove around for years when I first began farming. I was on a serious budget, and it helped that I could go almost two weeks on a single tank of gas. Over time the car developed a few mechanical issues that I repaired, but eventually these Michigan winters rotted the fuel lines. I resolved to drive my old Chevy pickup instead and put the Honda up for sale as is.

It was springtime, and Jeana and I were enjoying a balmy evening in the backyard while grilling our dinner. It was at that moment when

I received my first phone call about the car. The man seemed interested and said he could do the work and fix the car. I wasn't asking much for it, about $500, so I thought we would strike a deal. However, the conversation went from *sale* to *trade* in a hurry, and I realized that his high level of interest was really desperation. I finally asked him for some details on his personal situation. I learned he was a father of a young family and that he and his wife were both working but had only one semi-reliable vehicle.

My wife overheard the entire conversation, and I could tell by the look on her face she wanted to talk to me. So as he brainstormed to find something to trade that would pique my interest, I offered to call him back.

I know this woman—she and I have been together a long time. Before she could speak, I said, "You want me to give him that car, don't you?"

She nodded.

I laughed out loud. "Why is it that we are always giving *my* stuff away?"

We both laughed.

I called the man back. If you have ever given a stranger a gift, you will understand what happened next. At first he asked if I would take X, Y, and Z on trade.

"No. We are just going to give you the car."

Silence. "You mean for free? Don't you at least want the stuff?"

I said no, and there was more silence. We made pickup arrangements.

As I hung up the phone, my wife grabbed me by the hand, pulled me close, and said, "This is why I love you so much." She often saves her praise of me for times of maximum impact, so that statement by itself would have been enough reward, but the story is not over. God doesn't trickle blessings on us—he showers them.

About a week after they picked up the car, I was perusing online ads, looking for deals on farm equipment that I couldn't pass up. I had been hoping to use the proceeds of my car sale to help purchase a heavy-duty flatbed truck to haul hay with, but the farm account was pretty dry. I had just $750, and you can't buy much of a truck for that kind of money.

I stumbled across an ad for a truck with no picture. The seller was asking $1,500, and while I had nowhere near that much, I messaged the seller to see if he could provide any pictures. I was amazed at its condition. My mind raced to how I could obtain enough money.

As the week went by, I gave up on the idea. I didn't have any hay left to sell, and I didn't think I should sell any of my cattle to buy a truck I wasn't sure I needed.

That was when the seller called. He asked if I had come up with any additional money, and I said I had not. He then informed me that he was moving the following week and would take $750!

That truck often reminds me of God's investment in me and how I cannot outgive him. Almost every time I drive it, people compliment me on its condition. They are amazed even more when I tell them the story of what I paid for it. Wasn't I supposed to be the giver?

I believe that his blessings for me don't end there. In fact, I believe that the truck is just the part that's easy to see. The larger part is what that truck has done for my business—the time I have saved with it, the deliveries I have made with it, and the relationships that have developed because of it. All of this because of one small sacrifice I made. A sacrifice that at the time seemed so big, in the end so small.

When we invest ourselves in others, it takes time, energy, and sacrifice. But it pales in comparison to the sacrifice that God has made for us. If I'm being honest, I would have to say that I don't always recognize these opportunities. But I wish I did. Not because of how God will bless me, but because I love to show others the bounty of a loving God. I know what it meant for those people to receive that gift. When they came to pick that car

> When we invest ourselves in others, it takes time, energy, and sacrifice. But it pales in comparison to the sacrifice that God has made for us.

up, I could see it on their faces. It was in that moment that I was able to be the vessel of God's love for them, and it was my privilege.

These times, these moments are indeed the test. The test to see if we will remember the sacrifice Christ made for us. The time to remember that "our" things are really God's things.

PRAYER FOR CHANGE

God, help me reach your people with investment. Not only with my finances and gifts but also through the investment of time, through listening, understanding, and encouraging. Help me to give people the hope that can come to them through the blessings you have given to me. I know I can never outgive you. Amen

CHAPTER 6

Kindness

IF I COULD CHOOSE THREE WORDS that I would hope you would say about me, they would be, "He is kind." I hold kind people in the highest esteem. It is true that if we look at the actions of Jesus Christ in the Bible, they could certainly be described as kind. But I also believe that it is the best descriptor of his actual character. More to the point, if we profess to be Christians by definition, we would not only reach more broken people with acts of kindness, but kindness should also be the definition of our personal character. As Christians, our goal is to exude it to the point others are clear that they are talking to a follower of Jesus Christ.

The culmination of all the previous chapters in this book should point you toward kindness. I want it to pour from my body. I want you to see it in my eyes. I want you to feel it, whether I am hugging you, shaking hands, or just standing in your presence. When I get old, I want you to see kindness in my eyes and in my wrinkled leathery skin and in your memories of me. I want it to precede my arrival. For people to expect it from me.

Do people perceive you as kind? How important is kindness to you?

In Romans, Paul speaks of how God's kindness and generous patience leads us away

> Do people perceive you as kind? How important is kindness to you?

from judgment and toward repentance. Indeed, a great definition of "kind" is having a "generous heart." There is no better way to express to others that we are born again!

Romans 2: 4 (NIV) says that "God's kindness is intended to lead you to repentance." It amazes me how tough Christians can be on both other believers and non-Christians. Earlier in the same chapter Paul takes aim specifically at the danger of accepting the kindness given to us via salvation and returning it with the judgment of others. This realization is intended to be transformational.

> Judgment = risking the wrath of God
> God's kindness and mercy = our repentance and growth
> Our repentance and growth = kindness and mercy to others
> Kindness and mercy lead others to God and to repentance and avoiding judgment!

You can see how Christianity can spread rapidly according to God's plan of mercy. Repentance is the precursor to change. We must realize our faults and repent before we are able to grow and become born again. When we show others kindness, it leads them down the same path and shows them a new way—God's way of forgiveness and grace.

As parents, we want nothing more than for our children to be kind to each other. As our Father, God expects the same of all of us. My wife and I stress the importance of kindness to our children. We talk about what it looks like and how we show it to others. Kindness is never wasted, even on those who reject it. It says everything about the person *you* are and almost nothing about the person to whom you are being kind. People need not be worthy of it to receive it. In fact, oftentimes the less worthy they are of it the more it means to them.

Kindness is a character trait that each of us can carry and still remain unique. It is a thread that weaves through each of us in a different way. It's like having different brands of something you love. Each of us has a brand, one that includes kindness.

My kids each have their own brand. I have seen it grow and change and develop along the way. A few months back I could see some real changes coming in our daughter.

CASTING THE LINE

I recently started a post about my daughter:
What's your brand?

She's unique, not just in the way she dresses or the activities she enjoys . . . I have to say, if I wasn't her father, I would still want to be her friend. We've talked a lot lately about the "Madison" brand. We've talked about how the choices you make determine what you look like to others. We've talked about what it means to be kind and have great character.

After I wrote it, she did something that surprised me. I thought maybe she would look at it as embarrassing, as some children do when their parents acknowledge them. But she looked at it in the way that I intended it, as an encouragement.

I may not have mentioned, but I began my writing career on social media, slowly gathered a following, and started blogging before being led to write this book. Somewhere in my pursuit of writing, something I wrote (possibly something about her) must have struck a chord with her.

One day I came home from driving the bus to find that she had hacked my page and had written a tribute to me that was most flattering. In her slightly awkward but heartfelt post, I heard her encourage people. She encouraged them to be more like her dad. I cried. Not just because of what she said, but because I could hear her brand and my heart woven together. I was proud, not for myself and the things she had said about me to others, but because she was using her own words to express herself in a way that showed how much she valued kindness. She concluded her tribute with one of my own favorite endings.

Love one another.

I can see the golden thread of kindness weaving its way through the character of my children. They are bright and talented, but not one other accomplishment they have achieved has made me prouder.

Kindness is what I want most for them and for you. Think of the people who have done the most for you. Think of the times when you received a blessing you did not deserve, and you will understand the value of kindness. It is the meat and potatoes of Christianity. It is one of the fruits of the spirit and the magnet that draws other broken fish to you. Recently when I have struggled with being or acting kind, I have chosen silence as an alternative. In my silence I pray for the right words to say. Sometimes I need to walk away and return to a conversation or relationship when God has moved in my heart or in the heart of the person with whom I was struggling. Both of these choices are better than moving forward without the benefit of kindness.

One of my good friends is the most kindhearted person. While she sometimes struggles to create healthy boundaries, her impact on people is profound. People know that they can rely on her perspective without her passing judgment on them. Kindness, your outward kindness, is the reason the people will call on you in distress. It creates the opportunity to give of ourselves. It is the primary focus and gaze of the master fisherman, and it is the difference between casting a single line and throwing a large net. Do you recognize your own brand or style? What words will you choose to show kindness to others? What actions define kindness to you? Who do you think needs kindness the most?

> Think of the times when you received a blessing you did not deserve, and you will understand the value of kindness. It is the meat and potatoes of Christianity.

PRAYER FOR CHANGE

God, please teach me to be kind. Nothing I can do shows people that I am a follower of Jesus more than kindness. Help me to show kindness in both my words and my actions to bring other broken people to you and to repentance. Amen

CHAPTER 7

Humility

IN THE PREVIOUS CHAPTER I SPOKE about having a brand. One that is unique and special, one in which we can take pride. But there is a trap here, a trap that most Christians fall into almost daily. When we come to the realization that God has created us uniquely and wonderfully, it often gives us a superiority complex. Do you feel like God loves you individually and specifically? You should. And while each of us is supposed to feel the direct and specific love God has for us, we must come to the realization that this love existed before this revelation, before we knew him, and continues regardless of any kind of merit or action. It is unchanging and unbiased—for everyone. His love is unique to you and yet equally unique to everyone. How can this be? If you have children, you may have an inside understanding of this concept.

I have three children. Stewart, the reserved and respectful eldest son. Seth, my bighearted, ready-to-laugh middle child, and Madison, my witty, clever, and musical youngest. I hope you can sense my unique adoration for each of them.

Stewart is a thinker. Even at an early age, he was processing huge concepts in his mind. At five years old, on the way to school, he asked me about the internal workings of the engine of the truck I was driving. Being slightly naïve to the level of his intellect, I attempted to give him a ten-second scaled-back version of the internal combustion engine. Not good enough!

He looked at me and said, "No, Dad, tell me the whole thing." Five minutes into a longer, more detailed version, he seemed satisfied.

Sometime after that moment, I wondered how long I would stay ahead of him academically. I admire him more than he knows. His ability to harness abstract and complex thoughts and organize them in his head far exceeds mine.

Seth (the Bear), whom you will read more about later, is a lover. He needs and craves human connection. He loves having good relationships, he constantly battles with me over which of us is the best at making puns, and he is always ready for a hug. He leads with his heart. Every day he asks his mother if she needs help with anything. He is hard working and dependable.

And Madison, last and not least. I struggle to find appropriate descriptors for this girl. Of course, I love all the things I mentioned about her in the previous chapter, but in addition, she is wholesome and fun. She writes music and loves to entertain people.

They are my example and almost perfectly represent the uniqueness I am speaking about. My love for them does not depend on their qualities or their abilities. It is a constant and will remain the same for them regardless of status, orientations, beliefs, or politics.

To put this in better terms, God's love for us and for others is both equal and constant. Equal for each of us, regardless of our love for him, our following of his commandments, or even our knowledge of his existence. Constant and consistent, from the moment we are born to our last breath and beyond. Subconsciously, I believe we Christians feel superior to nonbelievers. I personally have focused on trading this superiority for humility. Being humble about your salvation and relationship with God is much more of an attraction. It draws people toward faith in a way that is inclusive rather than exclusive. For most, it would seem only natural to feel that God prefers us because of such an unbelievable gift of grace. But that superiority is completely manmade, and in it there is danger.

There are times when I'm guilty of this and times where I've been on the receiving end. I have friends and family members who study the

Bible daily. Some of how I feel about them might stem from me not reading it enough, but other times I can detect a blatant superiority complex being pushed my way. I've even heard the words "he doesn't

> Being humble about your salvation and relationship with God is much more of an attraction.

spend much time in the word [Bible]" in reference to me. I have never been more turned off by Christianity than in those moments, and I have sworn that I will do my best to avoid ever giving people that impression.

CASTING THE LINE

I reached out to a local business owner who had expressed that they were struggling to make ends meet due to the COVID-19 pandemic. I could tell from the desperation in one of his social media posts that God was indeed working on his heart, and he even concluded his paragraph by pleading to God for help.

I offered to write a post for his restaurant's page. He accepted. As eloquently as possible, I expressed to his audience the desperation they were facing. I made this offering to him as a cut and paste, removing my name altogether. I even suggested adding a picture, something with the owners' faces on it. In the days that followed, that post was shared almost a thousand times. In those first few days of its publication, the restaurant often sold out of food before closing.

It was exciting to see, so I reached out to him to see how things were going . . . once, then twice, without a reply either time. Not a "thank you" or a comment of any kind.

Now I could choose to be offended, but several scenarios played out in my head until I was led to following conclusion. God is in a different place with him! From there I easily could have made a jump to feeling superior. God somehow loves me more because of the lessons I have already learned. In some way I am superior to this person in his eyes. I could condemn this person (as in, offer my judgment upon him) for not offering so much as a thank-you.

There are a million times that these same story lines play out in our lives. They are so subtle that we can hardly detect their presence. Times when we use our judgment of others, and their situations, to make us feel special or superior. But our halo is crooked too! When we focus on the lesson God is teaching us, rather than the lesson we are trying to teach to someone else, we can view others as better than ourselves. As always, the Bible provides a perfect reminder in Matthew 7:5 (KJV): "Thou hypocrite, first cast out the beam out of thine own eye; and then shalt thou see clearly to cast out the mote out of thy brother's eye."

This passage reminds me of two things. First, God reminds me of my own sin and to focus on my own behavior, and second, that the only way for me to help anyone else is by living this example. Again, the wrong words could have easily cost me my future influence on this man and those around him.

Do you see yourself being caught in this trap? How can you learn to spot it ahead of time? How does it feel when people judge your behavior? Do they gain or lose influence with you?

PRAYER FOR CHANGE

God, help me change the way I think about others. Remind me daily that I am uniquely cherished by you, but that you cherish everyone just as a parent loves each child. Help me to stay focused on my own behavior to save me from passing judgment on others. Amen

CHAPTER 8

Anxiety

THERE IS ONE COMPONENT OF OUR behavior that is often overlooked. Sometimes I am not sure of the extent that I recognize it, even in myself. It may indeed start with one of the personality influences listed in previous chapters, but it is more than just the influences and characteristics of our personal situations. It has everything to do with our genetics, our learned behaviors, and possibly even the food we eat or the drugs or medicines we take. It is, of course, anxiety. I have in recent days examined my habits, trying to determine how many of them are even slightly driven by this hidden monster. Anxiety is a form of fear. Outside of love, fear is the biggest motivator in our lives. When the Bible says that "for God has not given us a spirit of fear, but of power and of love and of a sound mind" (2 Timothy 1:7 NKJV), anxiety is likely the type of fear it is referencing.

Anxiety permeates the world around us, and if we ever had a reason to carefully weigh and wield our words, it would be to combat the anxiety of others. It entwines itself with our identity, it is spiritual warfare at its core, and it works directly against the purpose and path God has for us.

What causes you the most anxiety? How is it holding you back from your God's purpose for you on earth? I personally have a list, one that includes even the decision to write this book. To others, my shortcomings and faults may be easy to overlook or even forgive, but to me . . . they are mountains. Likewise, in my eyes, your sins seem minuscule, but the perception of others does not diminish their impact on you.

We all have a list of fears. Some of them are healthy and are instinctively part of our self-preservation. Others are fears based on our perceived realities and only serve to control us mentally, or even make us physically ill. People tend to hide their greatest fears. If they share them with you, please handle them with the utmost care. If someone is vulnerable enough to share their weakness, you have a huge opportunity to win their trust. Do not waste it! You have a chance in this moment to drive away an anxiety that may have affected them their entire life. In that moment you have a chance to metaphorically land a trophy fish. With your help they could take a quantum leap forward in their relationship with God. In truth, their very salvation could be in the balance.

CASTING THE LINE

A while back, a classmate I hadn't seen or talked with since high school sent me a message. He was recently out of federal prison. While I need to keep the details of his situation private, his arrival in federal lockup started long before he was convicted. It started over forty years ago. I am certain from the description of his childhood, that it was emotionally and physically traumatic. Further, all through school he was bullied and harassed. Even being in the same grade, in a rather small school, with a graduating class of about a hundred, there were incidents that I had no idea were happening. I am ashamed that I was so unaware of what he went through.

> If someone is vulnerable enough to share their weakness, you have a huge opportunity to win their trust. Do not waste it!

From listening to his story, I discerned that his awkwardness and inability to fit in at school stemmed from his abuse and lack of normalcy at home. Confused by the mixed signals and the frustrations, he later turned to drugs. He attempted suicide by overdose several times.

But this was just the beginning. A drug habit this severe was expensive. He did not share some of the terrible things he did to support his habit, and regret would not come close to describing his remorse. In the end, dealing drugs would lead him to a life-saving decision. He unknowingly sold to a federal agent. While in prison, he contracted COVID-19, and lacking the strength to climb to his bunk, he endured most of it on his mattress on the cell-room floor.

What happens when you listen and empathetically understand?

I have a hard time imagining a scenario that would leave someone more broken. But inside, something happened. God found him on the end of his rope. Completely broken by a life full of trauma, he changed. He forgave people who had abused him. He felt the peace that only God, through such forgiveness, can give. Today, in his voice I hear a new man. In his voice I hear the freedom of his decisions. I am certain that now, in his late forties, the life that he has always wanted, and never understood how to achieve, lies before him.

Our conversations have been rewarding, maybe even more for me than him. So what have I said to him to make a difference? Very little, and I spent much time choosing those words. I have mostly listened intently, using my own experiences, not to compare to his but to understand him.

What happens when you listen and empathetically understand? What happened when I saw him as God would have me see him? It allowed me to speak with him without condescending remarks or judgment. It allowed me to focus on the words God would have me use.

Can you imagine living with this man's anxieties?

At a young age, he more than likely saw a skewed and perverse version of the world. He even expressed to me that he was confused enough to believe this abuse was normal to experience. Anxiety over future trauma would reign over his young life. It would be exacerbated even more during grade school, where he wore a smile on his face to cover the turmoil inside. This fear led him to substance abuse and eventually to addiction.

My friend is two years sober now. He has a great job, and he is thriving. But he and I have talked about the anxiety and guilt he feels. He has forgiven so many others, but he struggles to forgive himself. When you have truly forgiven the transgressions of others, guilt is the devil's last foothold. We all share this part of the story with him to some extent. We all share the guilt and shame from things we have done. What is the voice that tells us we are not good enough?

The answer is, of course, anxiety in one form or another. To understand your anxieties is a large piece of understanding yourself. When we forgive others and forgive ourselves, mountains are moved and a new path, God's path, emerges. When we bravely realize our sins and ask God to forgive us, we can move forward without shame. This concept is most important! If you want proof of this concept, look no further than the pages of this book. Without this forgiveness for both others and myself, they would not exist!

What anxieties are keeping you separated from the path God has for you? What is keeping you from realizing all of the abundance and gifts you have waiting for you? Do you understand to what extent anxiety controls your life?

PRAYER FOR CHANGE

God, help me to realize and understand my anxieties. Teach me how to remove them from my life, both through forgiving others and forgiving myself. Help me recognize and understand anxieties in others, both in the words and actions they choose, and show them your love. Amen

PART 2

The Life of an Angler

WE KNOW THAT WE HAVE A bias that exists because of the conditions we grew up in, but how does that affect others? How do we understand how to help other people? Do you know yourself? The obvious answer is, "Of course." But do you know who you are based on the conditions of your life? Do you know how it compares to the "normal"? How it compares to God's plan? Do you understand your own bias?

Who we are has everything to do with how we end up treating other broken fish. So how do we learn to understand where we fit into the lives of those people? We look more closely at ourselves.

CHAPTER 9

Deeper

I WAS RAISED IN A FAMILY with three sisters. Growing up, my father was an amazing but busy real estate agent. His father had died young, and therefore my dad, after age eight, was raised by his mother and his aunts. Because of this, he was never taught some things that only a father can teach a son. And though he has nurtured me more than he was nurtured, my mother handled many typically fatherlike roles. She and I shared an interest in baseball. She was the driving force for my love of the game. She played catch with me, drove me to practices and games, and even watched baseball on TV with me.

Much of who I am today I credit to my mother. So many discussions about life came from her tossing that baseball back and forth with me. She has an amazing understanding of people and a unique intuition when it comes to children. While this is only one tiny facet of my upbringing, how do you think it changes my perception of the world? How might it change the way I interact with others? This is part of my bias.

Having so much of my mother's influence has obvious benefits, but sometimes I struggle to understand the perspective of other men that were raised in "normal" or male-dominated homes. I did not understand this for a long time, and while I can never completely comprehend the paradigm of some men, I have better relationships than I used to because I now know myself better than ever before. Simply put, understanding myself has led me to better perceive the perspectives of others. Understanding myself has helped me become wiser in how I treat others.

So who are you? Which parent or role model had the biggest impact on your life? Who are they? Can you see biases good or bad that they may have handed down to you? Can you see what they are and where they came from? There are certainly perceptions and perspectives that began decades or even generations ago that still persist in people today.

There are many of these facets that play into your personal equation. Were you raised in a home that focused on financial success or maximizing family time? Did you have the influence of both of your parents, or maybe a grandparent who helped raise you? Did your family sit at the dinner table together, or did you eat all by yourself? Did you have siblings? Were they brothers or sisters? Were you treated differently than they were?

If we look for it, we can actually see personal biases everywhere. Our understanding of ourselves has everything to do with how we cast our line to the water. It has everything to do with how well we can help others. It has everything to do with what we compensate for and what we will pass down to future generations.

Do you see the problem? In today's society, we no longer look at ourselves—we instead point our fingers at everyone else. We only recognize our trauma for the sake of being a victim, when in reality it would make more sense to write our own story of victory over adversity. There is no glory to God and no joy in being a victim, unless it is used as a small chapter in a bigger story of triumph, a story that brings hope to people in similar circumstances. Imagine if Christ had just died on that cross and never rose again. Do you think he would have changed the world? Do you think his story would still carry on today? Where would the victory be?

Where is your victory? When we overcome and encourage others to do so, we steal victory from the devil and we begin to change the world.

What is the important part of your history? Who do you want to be? Do you recognize any negative influence of your biases on others? Can you see it in your children? Are you making changes that will bring them closer to a less traumatic, emotionally healthy upbringing? Are you healing the damage

Where is your victory? When we overcome and encourage others to do so, we steal victory from the devil and we begin to change the world.

from generations before, or are you perpetuating it? Exploring your personal history and recognizing your prejudices broadens your mind and opens up new ways of thinking. It changes the perceptions that you have of the world around you.

While exploring my history, at best I might have discovered half of what makes me who I am. I know some of the reasons that I succeed or fail with people and that there are many lessons yet to come.

Last summer I made a big mistake with one of my largest clients. Moments afterward I had a huge epiphany as to why. The story that follows gives you an inside look to who I am. It makes me feel insecure about who I am, but I am sure it is necessary.

I spend most of my summer making hay. Sometimes the crop belongs to me, as it is grown on ground that I have rented and sown. We either keep this hay for our cattle or sell it to customers for their horses or other livestock. Other times a landowner will hire me to harvest and bale their hay crop. These customers range from small landowners to large farms and dairies.

To give you perspective, my father did not farm. Ten years ago my wife and I purchased our first four head of cattle, and today farming is a major part of my personal yearly income. I have worked hard at becoming good at what I am doing, but I work in the midst of people who have been doing it their entire life. There are no places to hide when you are farming. Everything you do, every victory or failure, is being watched, or at least it feels that way.

Do you see that this might have more to do with how I see myself? Well, either real or perceived, this is my paradigm. I am a man among giants, trying to do what the giants do. I am in fact the definition of the word *underdog*. This bias would set me up for failure.

So what happens when you dwell on the fact people are watching you and you obsess over making sure that all of your customers have nothing but good to say about you? What happens when you worry only about doing the best job instead of focusing on the lives of the people you are doing it for? It doesn't usually end well, and what follows is a perfect example.

CASTING THE LINE

It was mid-June, and I was working at a fevered pace to satisfy my lengthy list of eager customers. One of my biggest clients and one of my smallest clients share a property line. The smaller client recently purchased a house and ten acres that ended up land locking the larger acreage behind it. Plans were made to create an access driveway, but in the interim I communicated that I would gladly either deliver the hay to the larger customer or would be there to lead them through the precarious access road to ensure that the smaller client didn't feel trampled on in the process.

Needless to say, when the time came, neither of those things happened. The larger customer, caught up in the rush to be efficient, accessed his field by crossing the front yard of the new owner's house, something that the new owner was not thrilled about and I had assured him would not happen. In addition, because the property had recently been split and there was no clear division or property line, hay that belonged to the smaller client got scooped up along the way. It was hay I had promised to a third party.

I was not happy. From my twisted perspective, this was just the thing to set me off. Did I recognize that I was seeing this situation through my own prejudiced scope? Did I calculate and approach with understanding?

No. In fact I did just the opposite. I made a phone call, and when the man responsible answered the phone, he was humble and realized that a mistake had been made. So what did I do? I made it personal. I spared him little in a blatant personal attack on his character. He ended our conversation graciously and continued to apologize and offer remedies. I hung up.

Immediately guilt covered me. I knew my bias had led me to speak in a way that was not congruent with my character. But it didn't end there. Within seconds my phone rang. It was one of the owners of the company. I knew what was coming, but I still answered. He had been in the room when the conversation happened. He had heard every word.

It wasn't just the owner on the other end of that phone—it was someone I respected, a good, God-fearing Christian man, someone who had offered me a job just a few months before, someone I looked up to and admired. In the minutes that followed, he expressed to me that an apology was indeed in order.

> It involves calling people up to what we would have them be, instead of calling them out for what they have done. It is influencing, uplifting, and unifying.

I agreed. And then he said something that I spent most of that summer thinking about. Words that were painful but helped me grow to understand who I was and, more importantly, why I am the way I am—words that gave me insight into my own perspective like never before. He said, "Maybe you're not the guy I thought you were."

Did I have it coming? I certainly did. I will tell you that many other people could have said the same words with less weight. I was devastated, not only because of my relationship with this person but because of yet another bias.

You see, right or wrong, I tend to look to strong male role models for approval, and I tend to look upon weak ones with disdain. I have no doubt that this tendency comes from my relationship with my own father and the fact that as a forty-five-year-old man, I still worry about meeting his expectations. Even though he and I have a great relationship, and we both have had many epiphanies about who we are along the way, I still cannot avoid the impact of his childhood and his upbringing on *my* life.

In the end, I made my apologies, and I spent most of the summer thinking about why those conversations happened and what they meant. Late in August I called the owner and told him what those words had meant to me. He too apologized, as I knew he would.

Since the day that made me realize that my personal experience was negatively affecting my business relationships, I have tried to change, to adopt a new strategy in similar situations. It involves calling people up to what we would have them be, instead of calling them out for what they have done. It is influencing, uplifting, and unifying.

PRAYER FOR CHANGE

God, help me to understand who I am. Not just my upbringing or my life's experiences. Help me to see who I am in relationship to others and how my story interacts with theirs. Amen

⚮ CHAPTER 10

Up

DOES THE PREVIOUS CHAPTER HELP YOU see me differently now? Do you have a new perspective? Can you see how knowing yourself can turn your weakness into your strength?

So how did I grow that summer? I learned the words I needed to say. But more importantly, I saw the kind of man I wanted to be. When we learn to call people up, not call them out, it is the difference between attacking a man's character and nurturing it. I needed to hear, in the moment I was at my worst, a kind voice say, "I'm not sure this is the man you want to be" or "This isn't the man I know you to be."

The man I had berated needed those words too, powerful words of influence, kindness, and grace. Imagine if I had called and expressed my concerns by saying, "I know you had the best of intentions, but this is not the impression that I can afford to give my other customers." And in fact, when I called to apologize, that is exactly what I expressed. This man had been in my shoes before. He knew why I was upset. He wanted to make it right, and yet my insecurities made it impossible for us to move forward.

> When we learn to call people up, not call them out, it is the difference between attacking a man's character and nurturing it.

Do you see the difference? In that moment I could have changed what I said from judgment to blessing, and in that moment, I would have avoided judgment myself. Think of how many times people in your life let you down, people that you don't even know. Think of what it might mean for someone who deserves your judgment to receive your kindness in its place.

Does the verse "Judge not, that you be not judged" sound familiar? The passage goes on to say that "For with the judgment you pronounce you will be judged" (Matthew 7:1–2 ESV).

The second verse no doubt is referring to God's judgment of us, not our judgment of each other. But ironically it happened in almost an instant that day, and it is a reminder for us to seek the grace that is afforded us when we know to call people up and not call them out.

Only grace saved the relationship between the three of us that day. I cannot put into words how thankful I am for that grace. I am a better man because of it, and I am sure this is just the beginning of the blessing that I will receive from knowing these two men.

So, do you see the parallels here? Can you see the connection between calling people up and encouragement and investment? They are, in fact, one and the same. Calling others up and not out is giving people love when they need it the most. It is choosing grace and love and perspective over judgment. It changes people. It helps them grow.

In the same way giving away a car brought our farm a blessing, calling people up to whom God would have them be brings blessings as well. Both the blessing of great business partnerships, as well as the benefit of those great personal relationships for years, and possibly generations, to come.

> **Think of what it might mean for someone who deserves your judgment to receive your kindness in its place.**

Calling people up is a show of grace, an influencing, unifying, life-changing principle that will divert you from the path of judgment and change the lens that people see you through. It is showing kindness when people sometimes least deserve it. It is the outward expression of thankfulness for God's grace in your life, and a chance for your character to shine. This is a chance that we cannot afford to miss. This is the difference between catching people in the net of God's kindness and telling the story of the one that got away. These are the opportunities that we miss every day, and they are the ones we should actively pursue. There are few better opportunities to bring healing to the broken.

Calling people up can be especially effective within your family and your children, the basis of which is laid out for us in Romans 4:17: "Speak of things that are not as though they were" (author's paraphrase).

And while there are many opinions about what this verse may actually pertain to, I have seen this interpretation work in my relationships in the following way.

CASTING THE LINE

People respond best when we reinforce positive behavior, when we *encourage* the behavior that we prefer. I have to say, I have seen many women struggle with this concept when it comes to their husbands, and to be honest, guys, we probably deserve it. I cannot count the times that I have done things trying to impress or satisfy my wife and had her say nothing to encourage my future behavior. Should it be necessary in order for me to do the things that I know I should? No, but it would make it so much easier to do them if she encouraged me.

Now, ladies, you don't have to overstate it or even reward it, but mentioning that you like a certain behavior almost guarantees it will happen again. Imagine if you came home and found the house clean and the laundry all done. You might be justified in saying, "It's about time you started pulling your own weight around here," or even something more pointed. But the way that we speak things into being is by saying something like this: "I know what it takes to do all of that housework, and I appreciate you doing it," followed by something like, "I love the man you are and the man you are becoming."

Did you catch it? How many things does that statement say? The first part says, "I've done this job many times, and I'm glad I don't have to do it today." What it does not say is that housework is a woman's responsibility. That statement leaves the door wide open for a man to do his fair share. The second part says, "When you do those things I feel loved, and I can't wait for you to love me more in the future." The future, the things you want, the attitudes and outlook you want toward life, these things are brought about more quickly if we speak of them as though they already were.

It's no different than making a plan for a vacation or writing a grocery list, but it is more powerful. Its power comes from speaking goodness into people's lives. It is encouraging what is right about them. It says to all of us, and especially to children, "I see you doing something great, and I know I will see more great behavior from you."

> Once you begin encouraging and speaking the behavior forward into the lives of people, the tide can swing dramatically.

The greatest thing about this concept is you only need a small opportunity to start something big. It can be as simple as recognizing a young man holding a door open for you or someone using good manners. This is calling people up on the smallest scale. Once you begin encouraging and speaking the behavior forward into the lives of people, the tide can swing dramatically. If you have never tried this approach, I implore you to adopt it and become an expert at it. The results are amazing. Without a doubt, it is one of the best ways to call people up instead of calling them out.

Do you see opportunities to call people up in your everyday life? Can you see where someone may have called you up and not out?

PRAYER FOR CHANGE

God, please help me to choose words that remind people of who they are and what you have called them to be. Move me to encourage the behaviors that you would have me foster in others. Amen

CHAPTER 11

Thieves

THERE ARE OPPORTUNITIES EVERY DAY TO steal from "thieves." In this context, thieves are people or circumstances that would turn people into victims and steer them away from the path of the angler and God's path. The devil, of course, is the biggest thief. John 10:10 (NIV) says, "The thief comes only to steal and kill and destroy." He will do anything to steal from us in an effort to separate us from God and salvation.

Most people, including myself, have a backstory that involves some degree of brokenness. When we use our story to inspire others to overcome their tragedies, we create an opportunity to teach them to become fishers of men. We give a gift that is contagious, a gift of freedom that they in turn can give to someone that they inspire. When we use our story of tragedy to inspire others, we steal victory from those would-be thieves. We replace a sad story of tragedy with something greater.

The following story is one that I love. It involves a young woman who chose to overcome, to be better and stronger, and to become the victor instead of the victim. Many of the lessons I have learned, God has brought to me through children and young adults. In my heart I believe he has used them to soften my approach. Without a doubt they have taught me patience and skill. These opportunities are all around us. If we were keener to them, I imagine we would see them daily.

Psalm 118:22 (NIV) says, "The stone the builders rejected has become the cornerstone." What a great example of how Christ's own story of tragedy stole from the master thief himself and secured victory over death and damnation. Think of what would have happened if Jesus played the victim. His story, and subsequently ours, would be dramatically different, to say the least.

So what story are you writing? Are you a victim or a victor? Will you use your own story to address the broken with compassion and understanding? The following is a story that isn't finished. It's about a young lady in the midst of choosing the story she will write. I am inspired by her. She is young, brave, and resilient. Her story is one of holding on, being patient, and staying in the game long enough to see God's plan play out. I am proud to know her and prouder still to be a little part of her amazing story.

> Think of what would have happened if Jesus played the victim. His story, and subsequently ours, would be dramatically different, to say the least.

CASTING THE LINE

She is tiny in physical stature, but I have never met a young person who understands the emotions of people so well. It amazes me how God puts so much potential in the smallest packages. If you think that maybe what you need to overcome is too much, I would beg you to consider her story.

This young lady first started riding with me when she was in the eighth grade. She was, for that year, the last one off the bus in the afternoon. Between the previous stop and hers, there were about two minutes for us to chat. Two minutes where she could express herself to an adult with no one else around to judge her. Two minutes to discuss philosophy, theology, or anything else that she believed in. It was in that small amount of time that I saw her story. It was in those moments that I gained perspective into her life.

She had it rough. In years prior, she had been splitting time between two parents, a condition that is tragic and difficult for everyone involved. But her story got tougher. She revealed over time that her father, plagued with bipolar disorder, eventually lost the will to battle and subsequently took his own life.

> So what story are you writing? Are you a victim or a victor? Will you use your own story to address the broken with compassion and understanding?

I was heartbroken for her. My daughter was just one year younger. I could not imagine sending her through her teenage years without my guidance and support. Without me there to tell her how proud I am. Or how she is beautiful and smart and worthy of great things, without teaching her how to be humble, and the importance of kindness, and all of the other critical pieces to a fulfilling life.

I decided right then a that I would involve myself in this girl's life as much as she and her mother would allow. There are times when God throws someone in front of you and says **Help them.** When he makes it obvious that he has chosen you specifically, it is most humbling. I was convinced this was one of those times.

Over the next year, things changed for the worse. The bus route changed, and I could no longer engage her with one-on-one time. I could see on her face that there was darkness in her life. I was scared for her. At one point I even said, "Just stay with me—this is going to get better." I was desperate to give her hope. The school year ended, but over the summer, I wondered how she was doing.

I didn't know it at the time, but I'd underestimated her. She was a fighter, probably more of a fighter than I am. I had never seen someone more determined to write the story of victory. I stand in awe of God's weaving with her. It's something I would be honored just to witness, and yet I get to be involved with it on a daily basis.

The next year I saw her change. She was initiating great conversations again, and she wasn't afraid to have them with other students listening. I could tell from these talks that she was forgiving her bias, loving herself, and stepping forward with faith. In just these few months, I could see her gaining confidence. She was seeing people how God sees them. She was actively pursuing the broken in her school and spreading light everywhere she went, an example of moving, tangible courage and faith.

Just before Thanksgiving she told me she was leaving notes and little gifts for people all over the school who she didn't necessarily know but who she figured could use a lift in spirits. I was shocked to find she had left me one that day. It was a Hershey's dark chocolate bar with a note attached that read:

> *Sometimes life can be pretty dark,*
> *But with great advice*
> *It can be a walk in the park.*
> *A bus driver who cares is pretty sweet,*
> *Thankful for you,*
> *Enjoy this treat.*
> *Happy Thanksgiving*

Being a teenager isn't the easiest time to show your faith in God. But she understands now that she has a gift that stems from her victory over tragedy. She is rare and beautiful, and she has a calling in her life, one that she intends to wholly fulfill.

So what small part did I do to help her to find the path that she is on today? I understood her paradigm. I looked at her like I would my own daughter. I tried to understand both the general insecurities that a young woman faces today and those specific to her personal plight. Did I say all of the right things? I am sure I did not. But I continued to pursue a relationship with her that revolved around the things I knew she needed. I told her the things that I would tell my own daughter, concepts that I thought would give her confidence. I spoke of things that are yet to come for her.

We invested time in each other, and over that time she began to trust the words of encouragement and influence that I had to offer to her. In that time, she encouraged me too, and I am a better man because of her influence.

There are times when we can personally choose the reaction that leads us to victory, rather than letting the thief rob us of our joy. But sometimes the willingness of others to be our advocate is the only thing that can save us. The influence of one strong individual can make all the difference.

I cannot wait to see what she does with her life—her story inspires me. Because of her personal victory, she will without a doubt teach others how to identify the thief. I'm sure she will recognize that particular pain. She can see the struggle in others. She can relate, and that ability is unique to a scant few people her age, and even more rare is her ability to embrace it and have plans to use it for the kingdom of God.

Out of the ashes of tragedy God creates the most wonderful stories. With faith that God has a plan for you if you only stay near to him, we thrive. In her story, I am reminded of Jeremiah 29:11 (NIV): "'For I know the plans I have for you,' declares the LORD, 'plans to prosper you and not to harm you, plans to give you hope and a future.'"

PRAYER FOR CHANGE

God, help me to grow and use my personal story, not of being a victim of my circumstances but a victor over them, as Jesus did. That others would see your glory in my witness. That it would be a testimony of healing that only comes from you. Amen

CHAPTER 12

Pain

I HAVE TO WARN YOU—THIS WILL be a hard chapter to read. If this book is about discipleship, then this chapter is about how desperately the world needs it. And I am not talking about just the nonbelievers or those in a faraway corner of the world. I am talking about those in our own backyard. Those who are struggling under the surface. The people straining to hold on and fight. *Depression* and *anxiety* are certainly mainstream terms used by celebrities and media to the point of cliché, but they are much more than talking points to those who experience them.

The price of missed opportunities can be so costly and painful. The first thing we often hear from the family or friends of a suicide victim is, "How did we miss this?" Other revelations include "I wish I would have said something" or "She looked happy." Please consider this statement—read it twice: Most people who commit suicide have come to a conclusion. They have already resolved to do it. They have thought about it, and they have planned it.

A suicide does not play out like you might think. The heroic television or movie scene where someone is talked down from the edge is so rare, I would dare say it almost does not exist. If your response to suicide is "I wished they would have called me or reached out," they don't. The prevention of suicide requires a preemptive, proactive approach. Cries for help are often masked or veiled, and we must learn to either spot them or engage with everyone to the point that they feel the compassion that prevents them from taking their own lives.

The following is a story about a young lady. My son has mild autism, and they were in the same grade together. She was a warrior, a defender of his. She stuck up for him and many others. My words fail to do her justice.

Her parents and sisters are loving and caring people. They and my son, as you can understand, were and are still devastated. Even years later, if I mention her name, my son still gets emotional.

CASTING THE LINE

For Holley

I have the privilege of being a father to Seth, a six-foot-four, 275-pound high school sophomore. At home we affectionately call him "the Bear." He has a heart bigger than his frame, but he isn't quite able to pick up on all the social nuances of kids his age. He sits in my school bus outside the high school every afternoon with the window open and says goodbye to just about every student coming out the door.

Last March he came home with a letter from the school informing us he had lost a classmate. Needless to say, he was heartbroken. I held the Bear in my arms (or he held me in his) while he cried. My wife and I consoled him, and we explained things the best we could. But how do you really explain suicide?

At about the same time, a heifer calf was born on our farm, and in usual fashion we asked the kids what we should name her.

"Would it be all right to name her Holley?" Seth replied.

Who was I to argue? Holley it was.

From the get-go, Holley was trouble. She was spunky and fearless. I came home from work one afternoon to find my wife out in the pasture, stuck in the mud, holding this calf in her arms, both of them shivering. I can still recall that the calf spent some time in our bathtub getting cleaned and warmed up, a night in our basement, and joined me in the kitchen for breakfast the next morning.

She's doing great now. But every day I see that calf, she reminds me that there's a struggle going on. She reminds me that there are so many who need our help. She reminds me even with great parents and families, our kids are dealing with serious issues. She reminds me that I personally and purposefully must be proactive in preventing tragedy.

They need us, all of us—they need *you* to step in, to be involved, to show them that they matter. They need *you* to ask them about themselves, what they like, what they want to do, how they see the world. Ask a kid a question, any question you can think of. Start a conversation.

> Our discipleship begins with the constant choice to engage people with words that project and emulate the love Jesus Christ has shown us. Because this is the definition of discipleship.

Don't just ask your kid—ask any kid. Ask my kids.

Show them that you *see* them, not just see them standing there. Show them that you see who they are, that they are unique.

Please ask them, for your kids, for my kids, for all kids . . .

Ask them for Holley.

When we stand before God, what greater task will we be judged on than this? "Whatever you do for the least of these you do for me" (Matthew 25:40, author's paraphrase).

Tell me, who is more desperate than these?

In the face of regret, there is one lesson that shines clearly in this tragedy: our discipleship begins with the constant choice to engage people with words that project and emulate the love Jesus Christ has shown us. Because this *is* the definition of discipleship.

So how do we begin? Let me start by saying that I should reread this chapter every day. The hustle of daily life makes it almost impossible to set our minds to see people correctly. To see people how God sees them. Our mental approach needs to change. Finding those on the edge requires skill. It requires changing things up a bit. Will you come out of your comfort zone to reach other broken people? Who do you see right now standing so close to that edge?

PRAYER FOR CHANGE

God, please embolden me. Make me both aware of the brokenness of people and more willing to act and reach out to them. Stir up my heart for those in pain and on the edge, and compel me to move toward them. Amen

CHAPTER 13

Genuine

IF YOU MEET SOMEONE ON THE street or on the telephone, how do you start the conversation? "Hi, how are you?" "Hey, how's it going?" These are great lines and express a desire for connection with others, but these phrases are a habit for sure. They are meant to express that we care about others. Of course, they can be used with sincerity and genuineness, but if we aren't pursuing an actual answer, then their purpose can only be to make us *look* like we care. Our language is filled with these clichés. Usually, we get caught up in what's "in" rather than something sincere. Ever catch yourself saying "whassup," "howdy," "yo," or any other slang when you approach people? What about just "hey"? Sure, it's widely accepted among friends and family and may even make us feel cool. But if we think about it, is that what we truly want or intend? As disciples, what we really desire is a genuine, purposeful, and intentional connection. In biblical times believers would greet each other with a holy kiss, and while bringing back this tradition in today's society may have its hurdles, I am convinced we could still manage to share a less physical but still meaningful greeting—one that expresses our love for God's people with both words and body language.

The young man pictured at the beginning of this chapter is my son Stewart. He is my firstborn. He is instinctively, and almost exclusively, a master of intentional conversation. He hardly ever just makes small talk. When he asks you something, he wants to know the real answer, and more importantly, he listens intently to your response.

The result? People know that he cares. He responds to them with kind, thoughtful words. I have never met an adult that doesn't love him. Even when he was young, he had more adult friends than kids his own age. Why? Because his motives were always pure and his conversations intentional and meaningful.

While his great character has been a blessing to us as parents, he has struggled with his peers because of it. At one point in middle school, he reported that some of his classmates were using poor language while in the dorms at a school retreat. In desperation to have him be relatable and liked by others, I suggested that next time he join them! He flatly rejected the idea, and to this day I don't think I've heard him swear more than once or twice. His character and approach to people may have been encouraged by his mother and me, but they are more reliably a product of his own God given compass.

Stewart has this same unique and thoughtful approach to his actions as well. He excels when it comes to gift giving. If you are ever fortunate enough to get a gift from him, you will understand what I am talking about.

We once had a conversation about whether or not the kids on the bus really liked me as their driver. Pursuant to this, for my birthday, he took a huge piece of paper, made a card, and drove nearly everywhere within a ten-mile radius of our house to have friends, family, coworkers, and even students at all the schools in our district sign it and wish me well! I am certain he had to push himself well outside his comfort zone to approach people who were strangers to him. He did this out of love and to show me how many people cared for me. I was impressed to the point to tears.

My point? Maybe it is time for us to abandon the clichés and use more meaningful greetings or actions. What sincere and original greeting is the best one for you? Maybe you could pick one that

> **Maybe it is time for us to abandon the clichés and use more meaningful greetings or actions.**

matches your personality? I am certain that there are some great ideas that are more unique and fun than some of mine. The following stories contain a couple of originals, and you are welcome to use either of them if they seem like a good fit. If we should ever meet, I would be flattered if you greeted me in a unique and caring way. Something that expresses a longing for a more meaningful and less rehearsed interaction. Something resembling a disciple and real fisher of men.

CASTING THE LINE

"I'm glad you're here."

Four simple words. For the last few weeks, I've been saying that phrase every day. Saying it to coworkers, to my family and friends, to the students on the bus.

Why? Because I cannot think of a better thing to say to show people how much I value their participation in my life. Because I am thankful for them. Because there is a spot in this world made for them, only them, and without it, and without you, there would be a hole.

I think you should join me—you might be surprised at the reactions. At first people shot me strange looks (getting kind of used to it), but I can see from some of the reactions that some people appreciate and enjoy it.

Here are some tips:

You can't expect change if you merely rattle off a halfhearted greeting, like a recording. Try thinking about the person and what you value most about them.

Make eye contact. Eye contact, by itself, almost always confers a level of sincerity.

Be genuine and sound genuine. Pause and think about what you want to say and how you want to sound.

This is so easy to do once you get used to it—it's just four little words that could really make someone's day.

"I'm glad you're here."

What if we purposefully changed our approach to remind us of our true purpose? Think if everyone said these words and meant them.

What if every time you answered the phone, you said, "Hello, this is [you]. How can I make your life better today"? I've run with this one for a while, and the one thing that is consistent is the tone of the recipient.

Nine times out of ten, you are setting the stage for a great conversation. Follow up your greeting by listening intently to their words and by choosing heartfelt responses.

I hope you come up with something unique. While the best greetings may reveal much about our personalities, I am not sure that the exact phrase or action really matters, provided it shows sincerity. I hope you use it to remind yourself to truly care, listen, and respond compassionately. The opportunity this could create could be the bridge that shows one desperate person that someone is listening to them, that someone cares. It could be the one thing that leads them away from darkness and toward a loving and caring relationship with you—and eventually God.

Scared to be different? Me too! But be encouraged—God will not make a fool out of you! We must do this in order to be fishers of men. Think of the price we will pay if we yield to fear or complacency. Lives, and indeed souls, are on the line. Think of the connections you could make with God's broken people with just these few sincere words or actions. What would your response be if someone greeted you this way? What kind of greeting could you develop that would reveal your heart for people and set the stage for a great positive conversation and relationship?

PRAYER FOR CHANGE

God, help me to be intentional and genuine. Help me to speak in a way that people understand how much I care for them. Give me the courage to be brave about conveying your unique love to people, by the way I greet them and listen their responses. Amen

CHAPTER 14

Grace

MY PARENTS ARE GETTING OLDER—BOTH OVER seventy years old now. I am realizing new things about them. In recent years they have told more stories about their childhoods. Perhaps that is what we do in our twilight. Maybe it's a way of having our lives be understood and remembered.

My dad in particular has had experiences that vary from extraordinary to tragic. I gather that, from an early age, his circumstances were less than ideal. Around age eight and shortly after his father died, his mother moved to a new town. Circumstances beyond his control kept her from enrolling him in his new elementary school, so he ended up walking to school and enrolling himself. Can you imagine that with your son or daughter today?

Many times, he has told stories of the things that he did "on his own," including walking at high school graduation without his mom there to see him because she'd had too much to drink that day. Of course, no one celebrated him with a graduation party either.

When I think of him, "self-made man" comes to mind. He has a pile of great stories, like digging an entire basement for a house . . . with a shovel! He spent six years in the army reserve; drove dump trucks; built several houses; and for years was our township supervisor and was instrumental in the creation of a large township park, which is loved by the community to this day. In addition, he chose real estate as a career and was voted Muskegon County's Realtor of the Year because of his great attitude and rapport with people.

The key to most of his accomplishments, I believe, stems from the fact that he is hardworking, self-starting, and determined not to quit. He has persevered even when things are tough—one of the lessons he has taught me that I value to this day.

But as you may remember from an earlier chapter, the tragedy of some of his circumstances has left him ill equipped to guide me through some of mine.

In spite of these things, I stand here today celebrating my father. I have grown to understand him better. I have tried to see how God sees him, because in him I see myself. I see the burdens and story that he and I share. A story of overcoming, of persevering, of tragedy and deficit. And in that story I see the chapters that he has made one generation better for me, plus a chapter in which I will do my best to make one generation better for my children. I have seen what was stolen from him, and to a lesser extent, from me.

I understand why he feels the weight of his shortcomings with me. I know it from the sometimes-awkward relationship we have and that often he and I both lack the words to say. This took me probably forty years, but I have so much grace for it now. A grace that comes from understanding. A grace that comes with freedom and thankfulness, without a trade-off or price tag.

Which leads me to the hardest grace. Grace for ourselves. Our churches do such a great job teaching us to forgive others. To model grace to the world. It has taken some time, but I have forgiven some huge transgressions. Things that I will never speak of or write about, things I have never told

> I would encourage you to embrace the promise of Jesus Christ and reject any effort from anyone who attempts to keep you away, including yourself.

anyone. But grace for myself is hard to come by. I think my father would agree. Would you?

I mentioned this before, but it may be the devil's crown achievement to make us believe this simple lie. You are undeserving of grace. Did Christ not die on the cross for my sin? Are my shortcomings not covered by his sacrifice?

The proliferation of this falsehood is the basis for the Enemy's assault on discipleship. It is as if Satan himself is speaking the words: "You are not good enough, or discipleship is for someone better than you."

For me, this is the toughest grace. If it is for you or someone you love, I would encourage you to embrace the promise of Jesus Christ and reject any effort from anyone who attempts to keep you away, including yourself. Here is an early blog post that I wrote, which might help you put this in perspective. To me it explains how so many of us feel. It remains a favorite to this day.

CASTING THE LINE

My wife and I have been married for over twenty years. I have learned that I will never witness her more excited than when we are starting a project. She loves to work, and even more she loves fixing things up. I don't know what that says about me, but I don't know if it's possible for her to buy something

_____

God loves a fixer-upper too!

_____

that doesn't need a "little" work. We've learned over the years together that if we buy something with promise and put a little elbow grease in it, we can come out ahead (most of the time).

But recent realizations have led me to believe in a new theory of why we buy the "fixer-upper." We have often coined the phrase "making it ours" as a cute way of saying we are fixing it up. There is fun in knowing every corner of that old camper, or every stone chip in the paint of that new-to-you pickup you just bought. There is an intimacy you gain through that process.

God loves a fixer-upper too! For a long time in my life, I was waiting until I had all my problems sorted out before I felt like I could come back to him. I know for some this may seem silly, but I have to believe that someone out there is waiting for this same reason.

Don't wait any longer! God is ready to have that intimate relationship with you that only comes from letting him fix you up. Connect with the Healer and King. It's easy—just take a minute to offer up a little prayer.

In the end, let us be reminded that the salvation and grace we offer to others through Jesus must begin by accepting that grace he personally has given us. If we do not, we are wasting Christ's sacrifice on the cross. This is one of the subjects that I speak with other believers about the most. The Bible is clear—there is no sin that can keep us from him if we accept this gift, but we must choose to accept it. Grace for ourselves requires coming to grips with what we have done, repenting, and knowing that we are forgiven. Even if others do not forgive us. What guilt or shame do you carry? Do you struggle with letting Jesus carry that burden? Do you have more grace for others than you do yourself?

> God is ready to have that intimate relationship with you that only comes from letting him fix you up. Connect with the Healer and King. It's easy—just take a minute to offer up a little prayer.

PRAYER FOR CHANGE

God, help me to recognize the guilt and shame I carry. Forgive me for those things that keep me from a closer relationship with you. Help me to realize the gift and freedom that have been given to me by Jesus's sacrifice. Teach me to have grace for myself. Amen

CHAPTER 15

Nibble

SO CAN YOU DO IT? DO you have the heart for God's people? Do you understand why others behave differently and have different perspectives? Do you understand your own paradigm? Are you willing to take the time to invest in them and craft a lens that they will see you through? Are you ready to call others up and not out? In short, have you honed all of the skills to become a master angler? If so, then we only need to wait on God for the opportunity to speak his truth to others.

Even when we change one characteristic about ourselves, it can change the opportunities laid before us. God's timing is crucial. I am certain that sometimes he is waiting for our hearts or our perspectives to be in the right place. Pushing forward without it is disastrous. Sometimes, opportunities to witness are situational and immediate. Other times it will develop over weeks, months, years, or even decades. In my experience, it is most difficult to spot them. For you it may come naturally and easily. I personally have failed to recognize so many opportunities, to the point that I have actually prayed and asked God to help me see them more readily.

> Even when we change one characteristic about ourselves, it can change the opportunities laid before us.

For this reason, I don't think it is a coincidence that God some-times lays his plan before me in an obvious fashion. The following story is one such incident.

I had never before been a godparent. But I am today. Not for one of my seven nieces and nephews and not for the child of a lifelong best friend. I am the godfather of a boy brought to me from the worst of circumstances five states away and set before me at the house next door.

I cannot disclose the details of this special boy's past. But I can tell you his situation was national news and his parents have both been incarcerated. Custody was granted to his grandparents, one of whom a few years prior had purchased a summer home next door to our farm. In the years leading up to our introduction, this boy's grandmother and I became good friends. She often stopped by to chat while we were doing our daily farm chores or when calves were being born. When Mikey became involved, the chores became a group effort. When we first met, he was small enough to stand on top of a five-gallon bucket full of grain, hold on to my arm, and "ride" from the grain bin to the barn. We developed a special bond that revolved around learning life-related lessons, driving tractors, and his unending curiosity about the world around him. He is indeed a special young man, and I am not sure I can put into words how humbled I am to be chosen to be involved with him. When his grandmother asked me to be his godfather, I gladly accepted. Feeling the gravity of my responsibility to him and inspired to express my feelings, on the eve of his baptism, I wrote this:

Someday
For Mikey

Someday we may talk about how I became your "Uncle Matt," but today let's talk about gravity.

Someday we may talk about the tragedy that brought you to me, but today let's count the tractors.

Someday we can talk about your baby brother in heaven, but today let's water the cows.

Someday we may talk about all the hard things, like why you live with grandparents and forgiving the poor choices your parents made. But today we will take rides on the hay wagon and in the grain bucket and we will drive every piece of equipment I own. Today we will sneak up on each other and yell "boom" as loud as we can. Today I will throw you in the air and catch you, carry you on my shoulders so the cows won't get you, and teach you cool phrases like "We've all been there one time."

Someday I will explain how God covered you, rescued you, and dropped you straight in front of me. We will talk about how God smiled down on both of us and what he wants to do with your extraordinary life.

Yes, there are so many things to explain to you "someday." But today I am honored and humbled to stand with people who love you and to witness the power of your baptism. Today I choose to always love you, no matter what choices you make.

Today you and I together get one step closer to his plan, the intricate weaving he is doing in your life and mine. Today we will celebrate what we cannot yet see but are so certain about.

Isaiah 43:1 "Do not be afraid, for I have ransomed you. I have called you by name; you are mine."
Love,
Uncle Matt

In retrospect, this story paints an even more clear picture of God's timing and presence. In the end, I pray he will feel the love of Jesus and his guiding hand through his life. I pray for the people around him, that they would inspire him to grow to love God and people.

CASTING THE LINE

I can see myself in Mikey. No doubt this is one of the reasons that God has woven us together. He is ambitious and curious. He is constantly moving, growing, and changing. He wants to do things . . . immediately! I am also probably one of the most impatient people. As a boy I hated waiting for Christmas, my birthday, or any other highly anticipated event or holiday. To this day, I still don't like waiting. My poor wife has dealt with me begging for birthday presents early for over twenty years. She still gets mad when I pick up the boxes and shake them to try to discern what's inside.

I like to take action and move in my own timing. But I have come to realize how critical timing can be when it comes to others. So much can be said for how God has waited on me. The first forty years of my life story has been about him growing me into the place I am today. A place where I could see more clearly his plans for me. Can you see where God has been patient with you? Has your relationship with God changed as your understanding of him has grown?

> Your personal commitment to God's timing could make the difference between showing someone what Jesus looks like, and turning them off completely.

My relationship with Mikey is a sporadic one. Through the winter I am lucky to see him once a month. But not every story begins, moves, or ends in this season. Ideas must often marinate before they produce change. In fact, sometimes patience itself is the greatest kindness. Being patient is passive love that requires little effort. I have had to be patient with Mikey about many things. Many of our conversations revolve around reinforcing Grandma's rules. Certainly, there have been times where he has missed out on fun activities with Uncle Matt because of poor behavior with Grandma, but even in the last year, I can see his character and heart developing into something unique and wonderful. More often than we would admit, we as Christians shove people toward faith instead of walking with them. Discipleship is an endurance race, not a sprint. Your personal commitment to God's timing could make the difference between showing someone what Jesus looks like, and turning them off completely. When I personally run out of patience, I become the most frustrated. When frustration hits, we risk losing everything for which we are working. The phrase "patience of a saint" comes to mind. Perhaps you can think of a time when a frustrated or impatient person turned you away from something? Can you see God's timing in your own life? Where do you fit in the timeline of others?

PRAYER FOR CHANGE

God, please help me to understand and trust your timing in my life. Show me the ways that you work so intricately between my story and those of other broken people. Help me to be filled with gratitude and thankfulness because of your patience and timing with me. Amen

CHAPTER 16

Grow

JESUS DIDN'T VOTE. JESUS DID NOT run for office. I'm not saying that you shouldn't. I'm not saying that you should not have opinions. Personally, I have many. We live in a hyper-political and confrontational world. What we are witnessing today is the polarizing effect that comes from politics. Have you ever heard someone say that politics are the answer? How absurd!

Being political with people is fishing with dynamite. It leaves people more broken than before.

Love *is* the answer! Love is showing people Jesus. In order to reach the broken, it is critical that we put on love. Have you ever closed your eyes and prayed and felt the radiance of our creator shining on you? If so, you may understand how his love saturates the world around us. He is all of the missing pieces of your life. He holds the answer to every struggle. From his solid rock of love, he beckons and pulls you to him, and he stands in the same place during the calm silence of peace, or the roaring of despair.

If you understand his love, you understand that being political can never change the world. We will only bring peace one fish at a time. Who has best modeled the love of God for you? Was it a parent or family member? Was it a close friend or maybe even a complete stranger who showed you kindness? Are they the reason that you are a believer today?

For me, this person is my mother.

I was a stubborn child with a serious temper. I'm sure I was more than a handful. I have quoted my mother saying many times that I was a "difficult child but a wonderful teenager." In truth, I needed more discipline than she actually gave me, but I am sure she felt like it was enough, or even too much.

While I am sure much could be learned from some of the poor choices I have made, I think the biggest lesson came not from my actions but her reactions. She has always simplified her goal. "I am only concerned with your salvation," she said. These are more than words. They are a mantra, a theme—to me they are the embodiment of Jesus's love. Forgiving our mistakes, encouraging our growth.

Her love for me was and is still to this day a constant. It became my solid footing, rooted in Jesus Christ, modeled in front of my eyes. Was it perfect? Of course not, and yours will not be either. But was it effective? Very! How did she do it? Certainly, the chapters of this book should give you many clues. They are indeed a picture of both her and me. One Mother's Day I tried to sum up exactly who she is in my life.

She's Never in the Picture

I realized something today. I don't have nearly enough pictures of my mother, and even fewer pictures of her and me together. A deficiency that I resolve to rectify soon. But I am struck by the irony of such a statement, because in my world she is in the picture every day.

They say it only takes one person, one heavily invested individual in a child's life to make a difference. One person to keep you on the path, help you sort out your emotions, and tell you you're not crazy. It takes one good person to show you your value when you feel like you have none, to say "keep going" or to say "no" when you need to hear it the most. It only takes that one great person to lead us to God, lead us away from self-destruction, and do it all with love.

For me, that person is my mother. She is the biggest reason that I love my God, my family, and my life. So yes, she is in the picture in the biggest way possible. Happy Mother's Day, Mom. Thank you for all that you have already done for me, my wife, and especially my kids. Your influence has made such a difference to all of us.

I am certain that for each of us, that special person is someone unique. My sisters have different experiences and therefore may paint a different, but likely positive, picture of our mother. I'm not sure the exact portrayal matters. What I am sure of is that we must show people who Jesus is through love—to the point that people see Jesus when they look at us. This is the perspective a true disciple strives to achieve. A picture of kindness and grace. A picture of love.

1 Corinthians 13:4–5 (NIV) says, "Love is patient, love is kind. It does not envy, it does not boast, it is not proud. It does not dishonor others, it is not self-seeking, it is not easily angered, it keeps no record of wrongs."

Be encouraged!

We all have those people in our lives, in our families or church, who remind us of who we once were. I implore you to be the opposite.

One day while examining the effects of the negative people around me, I was inspired to write the following: "Do you berate a butterfly for the worm he once was? Grow, change, improve."

My mother taught me to praise what is praiseworthy. In addition, one of the lessons I have learned from driving the school bus is that we should always encourage the behavior we like. It is much more effective than punishment. Hebrews 10:24 (NIV): "And let us consider how we may spur one another

> What I am sure of is that we must show people who Jesus is through love—to the point that people see Jesus when they look at us.

on toward love and good deeds." People will start their walk of faith from different places. It is important for us to encourage growth rather than measure results.

CASTING THE LINE

Nearly fifty years ago, my father, grandfather, and great-uncle built the house I live in today. It was my childhood home, and when my parents were ready to move, my wife and I bought it from them.

We have made many cosmetic changes to make it our own over the last eighteen years, but most of the interior doors remain original. On the inside of the old pantry door, just off the kitchen, lies a hidden history. There, scribbled in marker, pencil, and pen, horizontal marks, paired with cryptic dates and names, reveal the growth of two generations. Woven between the heights of myself and my sisters, my own children, now fully grown, give their own contrast.

Is their growth a contest? My son Seth, standing at six foot four, would be the obvious winner, over both generations. Madison at a dainty five foot three (five foot four if you ask her) would be last. But how would this be fair? My son was given the genes required for height, while my daughter was not. Clearly they were designed wonderfully and differently, but both have matured according to God's design for them.

Likewise, I believe that God measures our growth. Is it a contest? It is not. Would it be fair to measure us all the same? Even locally there are places in this world that the word has not penetrated. I once spoke to a man in his eighties who asked me about cultivating a relationship with God. Would you tell him it's too late? Our starting place has everything to do with what is expected. Our faith is not a measure of our given gifts—more reliably what

> In the end it will be how much we grow toward him, through our interactions and the love and compassion we have for each other— and for all the broken.

we choose to do with them. Not likely a measure of status or achievement, but rather growth.

In the end it will be how much we grow toward him, through our interactions and the love and compassion we have for each other— and for all the broken. This love, Christ's love, standing on pillars of patience, kindness, understanding, hope, and encouragement draws us closer to him. The foundation for a love that is both life changing and sustainable. Each of

> "Understanding the brokenness of ourselves and others is the underlying foundation for adapting and equipping ourselves to be disciples."

us is living a different story. It begins when your eyes were opened and you recognized him for the first time. The ending will be a product of God's nurture plus your personal commitment to growth. The impact on the world around you could be significant, your story a prequel to so many others. Your faith, measured by epiphanies and spiritual growth, like lines on an old pantry door could have a significant impact on the people around you and be critical to so many other stories. It is our purpose, like it was my mother's, to encourage growth toward salvation, to be "in the picture."

Our dedication to understanding both other broken fish and ourselves is the directive of Jesus Christ himself. No one has ever understood us better. No one has ever fostered the growth and change we so desperately need and crave. How can we ever expect to change this world any other way? Let me go back to the beginning. It starts with understanding. Understanding the brokenness of ourselves and others is the underlying foundation for adapting and equipping ourselves to be disciples. It is the crucial connection that allows us to radiate God's love . . . to everyone! Changing the world then gains momentum with the words we choose.

Common words whether written or spoken are only brush strokes on a canvas. Your words are the color palette, but the way you brush them, your artistry, and therefore the quality of the picture you paint comes from inside. Ultimately those brush strokes come from how well we personally understand, and therefore convey, God's kindness and love to his children. Words chosen with love and care will move mountains. They will foster change in even the most desperate of cases. I struggle with finding the right ones more than you may imagine. I pray that God would give you the wisdom to find yours.

And finally shine! I hope this book leaves you filled with hope, love, and encouragement. I hope it shines light on your path of discipleship. It has been an honor and a privilege to live and to write it! Let me leave you with this last bit of encouragement from my favorite verse—Matthew 5:16 (CSB): "In the same way, let your light shine before men, so that they may see your good works and give glory to your Father in heaven."

God has made me a simple farmer, not a preacher or a scholar, but this book is what discipleship and salvation look like to me. This, in my humble opinion, is the love of God. I sincerely hope to meet you one day, or at least see the impact you have made on the world. Go out into this world, emboldened by the one who spared nothing to reach you. Go out with God!

"Go therefore and make disciples of all nations" (Matthew 28:19 ESV).

I'm glad you're here!

How can I make your life better today?

Matthew Stewart Simon

PRAYER FOR CHANGE

God, give me the vision and wisdom to see people how you see them. Teach me to better understand others and myself. Lead me into the lives of people who need you so desperately, and help me to choose the words and actions that would lead them to you. Nurture me and foster new growth in my life. Help me to fully receive the gift of salvation that you gave to me. Show me the way paint the picture of your love for all the broken. Amen

ORDER INFORMATION

REDEMPTION
P R E S S

To order additional copies of this book, please visit
www.redemption-press.com.
Also available on Amazon.com and BarnesandNoble.com
or by calling toll-free 1-844-2REDEEM.